DEADLY DISEASES AND EPIDEMICS

POLIO

DEADLY DISEASES AND EPIDEMICS

Anthrax

Cholera

Influenza

Polio

Syphilis

Tuberculosis

DEADLY DISEASES AND EPIDEMICS

POLIO

Alan Hecht

CONSULTING EDITOR
I. Edward Alcamo
Distinguished Teaching Professor of Microbiology,
SUNY Farmingdale

FOREWORD BY
David Heymann
World Health Organization

CHELSEA HOUSE
P U B L I S H E R S
An imprint of Infobase Publishing

Dedication

We dedicate the books in the DEADLY DISEASES AND EPIDEMICS series to Ed Alcamo, whose wit, charm, intelligence, and commitment to biology education were second to none.

Polio

Chelsea House
An imprint of Infobase Publishing
132 West 31st Street
New York NY 10001

Library of Congress Cataloging-in-Publication Data

Hecht, Alan.
  Polio/Alan Hecht.
    p. cm.—(Deadly diseases and epidemics)
   ISBN 0-7910-7462-5 (hc: alk. paper)
  1. Poliomyelitis—Juvenile literature. 2. Poliomyelitis—History—Juvenile literature. [1. Poliomyelitis. 2. Diseases.] I. Title. II. Series.
RC180.1.H43 2003
616.8'35—dc21   2003000826

Chelsea House books are available at special discounts when purchased in bulk quantities for businesses, associations, institutions, or sales promotions. Please call our Special Sales Department in New York at (212) 967-8800 or (800) 322-8755.

You can find Chelsea House on the World Wide Web at http://www.chelseahouse.com

Text design by Terry Mallon
Cover design by Takeshi Takahashi

Printed in the United States of America

Lake 21C 10 9 8 7 6 5 4 3 2

This book is printed on acid-free paper.

Table of Contents

Foreword

In the 1960s, infectious diseases—which had terrorized generations—were tamed. Building on a century of discoveries, the leading killers of Americans both young and old were being prevented with new vaccines or cured with new medicines. The risk of death from pneumonia, tuberculosis, meningitis, influenza, whooping cough, and diphtheria declined dramatically. New vaccines lifted the fear that summer would bring polio and a global campaign was approaching the global eradication of smallpox. New pesticides like DDT cleared mosquitoes from homes and fields, thus reducing the incidence of malaria which was present in the southern United States and a leading killer of children worldwide. New technologies produced safe drinking water and removed the risk of cholera and other water-borne diseases. Science seemed unstoppable. Disease seemed destined to almost disappear.

But the euphoria of the 1960s has evaporated.

Microbes fight back. Those causing diseases like TB and malaria evolved resistance to cheap and effective drugs. The mosquito evolved the ability to defuse pesticides. New diseases emerged including AIDS, Legionnaires, and Lyme disease. And diseases which haven't been seen in decades re-emerged, as the hantavirus did in the Navajo Nation in 1993. Technology itself actually created new health risks. The global transportation network, for example, meant that diseases like West Nile virus could spread beyond isolated regions in distant countries and quickly become global threats. Even modern public health protections sometimes failed, as they did in Milwaukee, Wisconsin in 1993 which resulted in 400,000 cases of the digestive system illness cryptosporidiosis. And, more recently, the threat from smallpox, a disease completely eradicated, has returned along with other potential bioterrorism weapons such as anthrax.

The lesson is that the fight against infectious diseases will never end.

In this constant struggle against disease, we as individuals have a weapon that does not require vaccines or drugs, the warehouse of knowledge. We learn from the history of science that "modern" beliefs can be wrong. In this series of books, for example, you will learn that diseases like syphilis were once thought to be caused by eating potatoes. The invention of the microscope set science on the right path. There are more positive lessons from history. For example, smallpox was eliminated by vaccinating everyone who had come in contact with an infected person. This "ring" approach to controlling smallpox is still the preferred method for confronting a smallpox outbreak should the disease be intentionally reintroduced.

At the same time, we are constantly adding new drugs, new vaccines, and new information to the warehouse. Recently, the entire human genome was decoded. So too was the genome of the parasite that causes malaria. Perhaps by looking at the microbe and the victim through the lens of genetics we will to be able to discover new ways of fighting malaria, still the leading killer of children in many countries.

Because of the knowledge gained about diseases such as AIDS, entire new classes of anti-retroviral drugs have been developed. But resistance to all these drugs has already been detected, so we know that AIDS drug development must continue.

Education, experimentation, and the discoveries which grow out of them are the best tools to protect health. Opening this book may put you on the path of discovery. I hope so, because new vaccines, new antibiotics, new technologies and, most importantly, new scientists are needed now more than ever if we are to remain on the winning side of this struggle with microbes.

David Heymann
Executive Director
Communicable Diseases Section
World Health Organization
Geneva, Switzerland

1

The History of Polio

It is likely that polio has caused **paralysis** and death for most of human history. One of the earliest written accounts of polio is that of the Pharaoh Siptah, who ruled ancient Egypt from 1200 B.C. to 1193 B.C. It is said that Siptah was stricken with a paralyzing **disease** as a young boy. The illness left his left foot and leg deformed. People of the time believed that Siptah was being punished for his father's sins because his father had overthrown the previous Pharaoh Seti II and seized the throne.

In addition to Siptah's story, the oldest identifiable reference to polio also comes from Egypt in the form of an Egyptian *stele* (<Steel>), a stone engraving over 3,000 years old (Figure 1.1). Sanitation was poor in ancient days, and therefore people were frequently exposed to sewage that contained bacteria and viruses, including the active poliovirus. In the case of poliovirus, the virus entered the sewage system because poliovirus passes through the intestines and into the feces after being contracted by an individual, and the feces contaminated the water. Interestingly, this presence in the sewage system actually helped to create immunity, thus keeping cases at a much lower level than what would be seen after the development of sewage systems.

Normally, when a person is frequently exposed to very low levels of a virus that would not be sufficient to bring about a true case of a disease, he or she will not develop that disease. This constant exposure will stimulate the immune system into making antibodies to the virus which will protect the individual. The immune system is discussed in more detail in Chapter 3.

Gradually, people learned to dump waste away from the drinking water supply, a measure that protected against diseases like cholera

Figure 1.1 Polio has plagued humans for thousands of years. Some of the earliest descriptive accounts of the disease come from ancient Egyptian *steles*, or stone engravings, like the one pictured above. This particular stele depicts the deformed foot of a man assumed to have polio.

and polio, which are often spread via contaminated water. However, low-level exposure no longer occurred, and thus people no longer developed immunity. The percentage of polio cases increased.

THE BIBLE SPEAKS OF POLIO

Many references to polio appear in the Bible. In the book of Luke, 5:18, the reference to polio is translated using the word *palsy*. "And, behold, men brought in a bed a man which was taken with a palsy: and they sought means to bring him in, and to lay him before him."

In English language translations of the Bible, the word "palsy" is used instead of the word "paralysis" because it is derived from the Old French word "paralesie" which actually means paralysis. Middle English shortened this into "palesie" which appeared as "palsy" in the King James Version of the Bible in the sixteenth century. Of course, today we use the word "paralysis" when referring to the result of an infection with the poliovirus.

Another reference to polio appears in the Book of Matthew, 8:5-6: "And when Jesus was entered into Capernaum, there came unto him a centurion, beseeching him, and saying, Lord, my servant lieth at home sick of the palsy, grievously tormented." Once again, polio is referred to in the ancient text.

Polio appears for a third time in The Acts of the Apostles, 9:33. Here, the permanent paralysis associated with polio is described: "And there he found a certain man named Aeneas, which had kept his bed eight years, and was sick of the palsy."

The Old Testament also contains references to polio. In the Book of Job, 33:19-21, a description of the pain and withering of limbs affected by polio is clearly described: "He is chastened also with pain upon his bed, and the multitude of his bones with strong pain. So that his life abhorreth bread, and his soul dainty meat. His flesh is consumed away, that it cannot be seen; and his bones that were not seen stick out."

A DISEASE OF CHILDREN

Polio generally afflicts the young. Although these biblical references do not specifically mention children, later historical accounts do. Sir Walter Scott (1771–1832), a Scottish novelist and poet, wrote about his own case of polio. His account, written in 1827, was the earliest recorded in the United Kingdom:

> I showed every sign of health and strength until I was about 18 months old. One night, I have been often told, I showed great reluctance to be caught and put to bed, and after being chased about the room, was apprehended and consigned to my dormitory with some difficulty. It was the last time I was to show much personal agility. In the morning I was discovered to be affected with the fever which often accompanies the cutting of large teeth. It held me for three days. On the fourth, when they went to bathe me as usual, they discovered that I had lost the power of my right leg . . . when the efforts of regular physicians had been exhausted, without the slightest success . . . the impatience of a child soon inclined me to struggle with my infirmity, and I began by degrees to stand, walk, and to run. Although the limb affected was much shrunk and contracted, my general health, which was of more importance, was much strengthened by being frequently in the open air, and, in a word, I who in a city had probably been condemned to helpless and hopeless decrepitude, was now a healthy, high-spirited, and, my lameness apart, a sturdy child. [1]

In 1789, Michael Underwood, a British physician, published the first known clinical description of polio as a "Debility of the Lower Extremities." Once again, the passage refers to children:

> The disorder intended here is not noticed by any medical writer within the compass of my reading, or is not a

---

1. Lockhart, J.G. *Memoirs of Sir Walter Scott.* (Edinburgh: A. and C. Black, 1882).

common disorder, I believe, and it seems to occur seldomer in London than in some parts . . . It seems to arise from debility, and usually attacks children previously reduced by fever; seldom those under one, or more than four or five years old. The Palsy . . . sometimes seizes the upper, and sometimes the lower extremities; in some instances, it takes away the entire use of the limb, and in others, only weakens them." [2]

In analyzing the content of Underwood's description from a twenty-first century point of view, anyone who is very familiar with polio can see that the description was technically accurate for a doctor of the eighteenth century. This is surprising since there was not much known about polio during this time. A twenty-first century physician could have written the account. Because polio has historically occurred more often in children than adults, the term "infantile paralysis" was originally used to identify the disease.

POLIO MAKES THE NEWS

Outbreaks of polio in Europe were not recorded until the early nineteenth century. In 1840, a German orthopedic surgeon named Jacob von Heine wrote the first detailed description of polio based on his studies of infected patients. His writings identified the spinal cord as the site of involvement, which we now know is correct.

Von Heine's description came only five years after small outbreaks of polio were reported in the United States and United Kingdom. Considering how little was known about polio during this period in history, von Heine's work was quite insightful and forward thinking. After his discovery, an

2. Underwood, M. A. *Treatise on the Diseases of Children with General Directions for the Management of Infants from Birth.* 2nd edition. (London: Mathews, 1789)

DID YOU KNOW THAT . . .

Jacob von Heine published a 78-page monograph in 1840 that described the clinical features of polio and also noted that its symptoms suggested the involvement of the spinal cord. The limited medical knowledge of the time and the sub-microscopic nature of the poliovirus kept von Heine and others from understanding the contagious nature of the disease. Even with the relatively large outbreaks of polio that occurred in Europe during the second half of the nineteenth century, physicians attributed the disease to causes such as teething, stomach upset, and trauma.

interesting pattern developed. Polio **epidemics** in developed nations in the northern hemisphere began to be reported each summer and fall, but not in the spring or winter.

The epidemics became more and more severe, and the average age of those affected increased. The number of deaths from polio began to increase as well. A disease that had existed for thousands of years in only a few areas, and that had affected a limited number of people, was now coming to the forefront in many locations.

It was not until 1908 that the Viennese immunologist Karl Landsteiner (Figure 1.2) and his associate Ervin Popper discovered that bacteria could not be found in the spinal cord tissue of infected humans. Perhaps, they thought, bacteria were not the cause of the disease. This led them to suggest that a virus was the causative agent of polio. Of course, without an electron microscope, they could not actually see the virus, but today we know that their supposition was correct.

A DYNAMIC EXPERIMENT

Landsteiner and Popper set out to test their hypothesis. To prove that a virus, in the absence of bacteria, was the cause of

Figure 1.2 Karl Landsteiner, pictured here in his laboratory, was one of the first scientists to hypothesize that polio was a viral infection. Prior to his studies, researchers believed that bacteria caused the debilitating disease. Landsteiner and Ervin Popper (not pictured) proved their hypothesis by injecting spinal cord tissue of children who had died of polio into monkeys that later developed the disease.

polio, they ground up the spinal cords of children who had died of polio and injected the material into monkeys. Soon, the monkeys developed the disease.

The following year, researchers Simon Flexner and Paul Lewis, working at Johns Hopkins University in Maryland, confirmed Landsteiner and Popper's findings. This was of great importance since scientists could now attempt to find a vaccine to stop the spread of this deadly disease. Flexner and Lewis were able to successfully transfer polio from one monkey to another. They started out the same way that Landsteiner and Popper did, by injecting diseased human spinal cord tissue into the brains of monkeys. Once a monkey began to show symptoms, a suspension of its diseased spinal cord tissue was injected into other monkeys. Because each successive monkey developed the disease, their work was considered a huge success.

After the success of the experiment, Flexner was quoted as saying, "We failed utterly to discover bacteria, either in film preparations or in cultures, that could account for the disease." Therefore, they concluded, " . . . the infecting agent of epidemic poliomyelitis belongs to the class of the minute and filterable viruses that have not thus far been demonstrated with certainty under the microscope." [3]

HOW IS IT TRANSMITTED?

In the meantime, it became extremely important to find out how the disease was transmitted from one person to another. Initially, Flexner and Lewis felt that polio was spread directly from the nose to the brain. They introduced washings from the nose and throat of infected people into monkey nasal passages. Because the monkeys developed polio, the scientists concluded that this was the **mode of transmission**. For more than 20 years, people believed that this was, indeed, the way to spread polio. Unfortunately, when scientists thought that this was the correct mode of transmission, they stopped searching for any other mode of spreading the disease. Later, it was found that this was not the route of transmission.

A hint as to the true means of spreading the disease was found in 1912 when Swedish researchers discovered poliovirus in the contents and walls of the human small intestine. At the time, nobody really knew that this was the real pathway of the

---

3. Flexner, S. and P.A. Lewis. "The Transmission of Acute Poliomyelitis to Monkeys." *Journal of the American Medical Association.* 53 (1909): 1639.

Figure 1.3 Albert Sabin was the first researcher to show that the polio virus was present in the digestive system, as well as the brain and spinal cord. Sabin, pictured above, developed the first oral vaccine for polio. Jonas Salk, who is discussed in later chapters, actually developed the first polio vaccine, which had to be given by injection.

virus. Unfortunately, because of Flexner and Lewis' work, it was believed that these intestinal viruses only existed because of swallowed nasal contents.

It was not until 1941 that a researcher named Albert Sabin (Figure 1.3) showed that poliovirus was not present in the nasal membranes of patients who had died. He was able to demonstrate the presence of the virus in the digestive tract as well as the brain and spinal cord. Other researchers were able to support Sabin's findings, and this led scientists to agree that polio actually began as a digestive illness.

Today, we know that the majority of polio cases actually do not cause **symptoms** in those who are infected. In about five percent of the cases, one of three sets of symptoms occurs depending on which form of the disease a person actually has. The three forms of polio are: mild polio, nonparalytic polio, and paralytic polio.

In a case of mild polio, a person will experience headache, nausea, vomiting, general discomfort, and a slight fever for about three days. These symptoms resemble a typical intestinal virus. Following this, the person will recover fully because this low-grade form of the virus is defeated by the immune system before it can develop into anything more serious.

In cases of nonparalytic polio, the patient will have the same symptoms as with mild polio, with the addition of moderate fever, stiff back and neck, fatigue, and muscle pain. No paralysis occurs in this type of polio. It is sometimes referred to as **aseptic meningitis** <A-sep-tick men-in-GI-tiss>.

Patients who actually develop paralytic polio will experience muscle weakness, stiffness, tremors, fever, constipation, muscle pain and **spasms**, and difficulty swallowing. These patients will most likely develop paralysis in one or both legs and/or arms and will be permanently disabled. Depending on the degree of paralysis, their disabilities will vary.

2

The Transmission of Polio and How it Affects the Body

On the beautiful summer day of August 10, 1921, a 39-year-old lawyer named Franklin Delano Roosevelt (known familiarly to the public as FDR) was enjoying a well-earned vacation on Campobello Island in New Brunswick, Canada. Unfortunately, he had just lost the election of 1920 as the vice presidential candidate for the Democratic Party. However, the lost election did not put a damper on his spirits as he and his three eldest children Anna, James, and Elliot, sailed around the island on his twenty-four foot sloop, Vireo.

After finishing their trip, they returned home for a two-mile jog to their favorite pond for a swim. When the future president returned to the cottage, he felt a chill come over him and was too tired to even eat with the family. He read for a while and went to bed with a sore back.

The next morning, he awoke with a fever of 102°F and aching, weak legs. As the day wore on, the pain in his legs spread to his back and neck, and eventually he was unable to move his legs at all. Until this point in his life he had been an active, healthy man who was used to exercising. Now, he would spend the rest of his life in a wheelchair, never walking again (Figure 2.1).

What FDR did not know at first was that at some point in the weeks before he arrived at Campobello, he had contracted polio. The

Figure 2.1 Franklin Delano Roosevelt, president of the United States from 1933 to 1945, is one of the many famous people who was afflicted by the disease. As can be seen in this photo of the former president, Roosevelt had to use a wheelchair after the disease damaged his legs.

usual incubation period for polio is three to 21 days, depending on how much virus the person is exposed to.

After several doctors examined Roosevelt and could not determine why he was not improving, Dr. Robert Lovett, a

Harvard specialist and an expert on infantile paralysis, was consulted. Sadly, he confirmed the family's worst fear: FDR had indeed contracted polio.

HOW DID THIS HAPPEN?

Naturally, everyone wanted to know: "How did he get sick in the first place?" It was known that the poliovirus could be transmitted through water, especially in the summer when people spent much time swimming, often in "water holes" that were contaminated by sewage. In an area where raw sewage is able to enter the water without being treated first, the poliovirus spreads easily. All a person has to do is swallow some of this contaminated water either from a drinking water supply or from a river, lake, or stream where he or she might be swimming. Once this happens, the virus infects the intestinal tract.

Once in the cells of the intestinal tract, the virus **replicates** <REP-li-kates>, or reproduces, making thousands of new viruses. These viruses are then carried through the intestinal tract and released via the feces back into the sewage system to start the cycle all over again. In addition to spreading through untreated water, the virus can spread through human contact, especially among children who often do not wash their hands.

DID YOU KNOW THAT . . .

Few Americans were ever aware of Franklin D. Roosevelt's disability. This was due in large part to the cooperation of members of the press who almost always photographed him from the waist up. FDR insisted on this policy when he re-entered politics after his bout with polio, and it was continued during his presidency. He felt that the nation should see him as a strong man with no physical problems. This would give the American people confidence in the government.

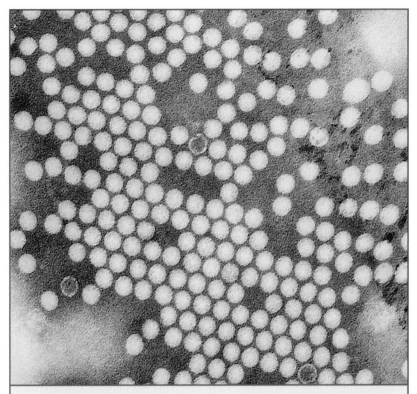

Figure 2.2 Polio is caused by the organism poliovirus. An electron micrograph of the virus is shown in this picture. The virus can cause symptoms ranging from mild discomfort and muscle weakness to total paralysis. Polio is spread through contaminated food and water but not usually through casual contact with an infected person.

CATCHING THE BEAST

Viruses are not as complex as animal and plant cells, or even bacteria. They consist of only genetic material and a protein coat. They do not have any systems such as a digestive or reproductive system. In order to replicate, they require a living cell that they can invade so that they may introduce their genetic information into the host. Poliovirus infects a person in the same way that other viruses cause infections. Humans are the only natural host for the virus (Figure 2.2).

When a virus enters the body, it will seek out cells that have specific proteins on their surface. These proteins are called receptor sites and act like parking spaces for the virus. As long as there is a place to park, the virus attaches to the cell and introduces its genetic information into the nucleus of the cell where all of the genes are located.

The viral genes become part of the host's genetic makeup and then direct the cell to act like a photocopy machine to produce millions of copies of the virus. The cell eventually bursts and releases the new viruses into the system so that they can infect even more cells. Of course, when these cells burst, there is damage to the tissue.

HOW DOES IT WORK?

In a case of polio, the cells that are infected are located in the anterior portion of the spinal cord. This area is used to send signals to muscles so that they can move. When these cells are destroyed, the muscles that receive signals from them in order to move can no longer function and paralysis occurs.

Once the cells of the intestinal tract are infected, one of several situations may occur. A person may be **asymptomatic** <A-simp-toe-matik> meaning that he or she does not develop the disease or show any symptoms. Or he or she may have mild symptoms that include a headache, fever, and vomiting for 72 hours or less.

If a person does develop symptoms, he or she may have a nonparalytic and less serious form of the disease. In such a case, the patient will suffer with diarrhea, a moderate fever, excessive fatigue, vomiting, pain, muscle tenderness, and spasms in any area of the body. These symptoms may last for up to two weeks and then disappear, leaving the patient with no further problems.

Approximately one percent of all polio patients develop the paralytic form of polio. These patients develop a stiff neck and back, fever, pain, headaches, and muscle weakness that comes on quickly anywhere in the body and may develop into

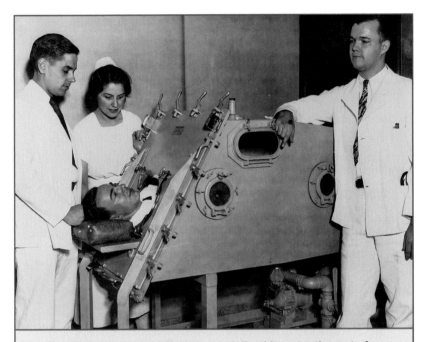

Figure 2.3 Polio can affect the medulla oblongata, the part of the brain that controls breathing. If this occurs, the patient may have trouble breathing or not be able to breathe at all without help. The Iron Lung, invented in 1928 by Philip Drinker, helps people who cannot breathe on their own. The machine encloses the patient from the neck down, forms an airtight seal, and regulates the pressure surrounding the patient's chest, thus aiding in the breathing process. The man in the picture above is using an iron lung to breathe.

paralysis. In addition, the person may have difficulty urinating and swallowing, muscle spasms, and trouble breathing. Up to ten percent of these cases end in death.

If the virus affects the cells of the **medulla oblongata** <med-DOO-la ob-long-GA-ta> in the brain stem, the structure that controls breathing, a person develops bulbar polio. In these cases, breathing becomes almost impossible without the aid of a device called an iron lung (Figure 2.3). This was developed by Philip Drinker in 1928 and was used for several decades to help people with bulbar form of polio to breathe. The iron lung was a large metal machine that helped to regulate the pressure surrounding the patient's chest, thus allowing air to be forced into the lungs of a person who could not breathe on his own. The patient was enclosed in the machine, from neck to toes, and an airtight seal was formed around the neck. Iron lungs are still used occasionally today to help people breathe.

THE TREATMENT PLAN

Unfortunately, as with most viruses, there is no actual treatment that will cure a case of polio. That does not mean, however, that some of the patients suffering cannot find some relief. In addition to using an iron lung, if necessary, to aid breathing, a patient can be given medicines that reduce the headaches, muscle spasms, and pain. If a urinary tract infection develops, antibiotics are prescribed. Physical therapy and even surgery may prove useful to help restore some of the individual's lost muscle function.

Sister Elizabeth Kenny (Figure 2.4) in Australia developed an interesting and useful form of therapy in 1933. She believed that the main problem in early polio cases was muscle spasms. She felt strongly that applying hot packs and using physical therapy was the best method to treat patients when they first developed the disease. This belief stemmed from her observation that Aboriginal children in Australia who had polio were treated with hot cloths.

During this time period, many doctors believed that **immobilization** using splints and casts was the best way to treat a polio victim. It is easy to see how a disagreement between Sister Kenny and the medical profession developed. In fact, one of her most outspoken critics was Dr. Robert Lovett, the polio specialist who had treated Franklin D. Roosevelt in 1921.

Never losing her determination, Sister Kenny did not get

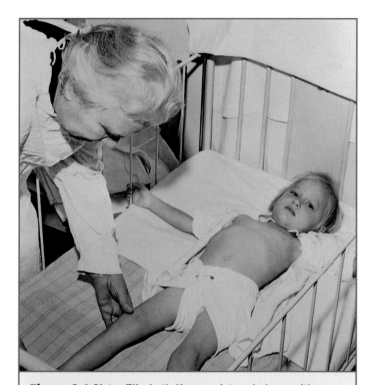

Figure 2.4 Sister Elizabeth Kenny, pictured above with a young polio patient, believed that hot packs and massages would help polio patients regain use of their muscles, a method she developed in 1933. Although her methods were popular in her native Australia, doctors in the United States believed in immobilization of the afflicted limbs. Kenny's technique was finally accepted as an alternative therapy for polio when she was invited to become a guest faculty member at the University of Minnesota in 1940.

angry. She opened the first polio treatment clinic in Townsville, Queensland, Australia, in 1933. Kenny persisted in her work and developed an attitude of understanding towards her critics:

> The American doctor, in my opinion, possesses a combi-
> nation of conservatism and that other quality which has
> put the United States in the forefront in almost every

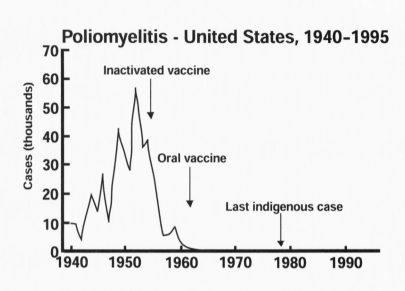

Figure 2.5 Since the creation of the polio vaccines (both Salk's and Sabin's) and nationwide immunization programs, the number of polio cases in the United States has decreased dramatically. As this graph shows, the last indigenous (naturally occurring) case in the United States occurred in the late 1970s. Polio still occurs in other places worldwide.

department of science—that is, an eagerness to know what it is really all about, in order that he may not be the one left behind if there is something to it. This eagerness, however, does not persuade him to abandon caution.[4]

Sister Kenny was well-received at the University of Minnesota and became a guest faculty member there. Many medical doctors set aside their differences of opinion and accepted her treatment methods because she had a good

4. Kenny, Elizabeth. *And They Shall Walk; The Life Story of Sister Elizabeth Kenny.* (New York: Dodd, 1943)

success rate in helping patients achieve partial recoveries. In 1943, she met with President Roosevelt and received funding from the National Foundation for Infantile Paralysis to be used to train Kenny therapists at the University of Minnesota.

Today, in the United States, polio is considered a disease of the past (Figure 2.5). This is thanks to the extensive vaccination campaign that began with the development of the Salk vaccine in 1952 and later with the introduction of the Sabin oral vaccine in 1962. Both vaccines will be discussed in later chapters. In the Western Hemisphere, naturally occurring polio has not been seen since 1994.

3

Vaccines and How They Work

Most children don't like getting vaccinated. "Ouch," they may say. "That hurts!" In the end, though, it is worth the discomfort. It would be safe to say that the development of vaccinations is one of the most important contributions to the survival of mankind (Figure 3.1). They have helped to protect us, our pets, and our livestock from many different diseases. Along with advances in technology and medicine, vaccinations have helped to increase today's average human lifespan to approximately 76 years of age. That is not a bad achievement, considering that at the beginning of the twentieth century the average lifespan was only 47 years.

THE BODY'S ARMED FORCES

In order to understand how vaccinations work, we must review one of the human body's systems that helps us to stay healthy and free from disease. That system is known as the *immune system*. The immune system is complex and includes several organs, specialized cells in our blood, and different chemicals. All of these parts work together to fight off attacks by bacteria, viruses, parasites, and other invaders. This system might be considered as the body's armed forces.

The skin acts as a general defender against invasion by physically blocking access to our bodies. When we get a cut or a scrape, the blocking ability of the skin is compromised, and we can get a localized infection due to invasion by **microorganisms**. It is at this point that more of the immune system goes into action.

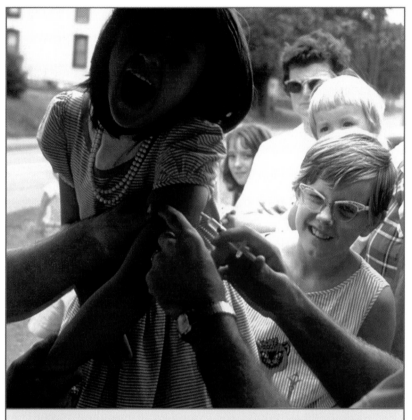

Figure 3.1 In the picture above, a young girl receives her polio vaccine. A nationwide program of polio vaccines has virtually eliminated the virus in the United States. Two types of polio vaccines exist: the inactivated polio vaccine and the oral vaccine which uses an attenuated virus. Both vaccines will be discussed in this chapter.

Special cells known as white blood cells (also known as **leukocytes** <LU-co-sites>) now begin to move into action. There are five different kinds of these cells that make up part of our immune system. Here we will focus on two types, neutrophils and lymphocytes.

One type of white blood cell, known as a **neutrophil**, is always found circulating in our blood. When the invasion occurs, special chemicals attract these cells to the site where the bacteria or other microorganisms have been allowed to enter. When they encounter the invaders, the neutrophils will attack by engulfing and digesting them. This process is called **phagocytosis** <fag-o-site-O-sis> (Figure 3.2). The neutrophil has a "cousin" called the **macrophage**. This cell also has the power to perform phagocytosis. Both cells are classified as phagocytes. In Latin, this actually means "eating cells" (phago = eating, cyte = cell).

Another group of specific chemicals called **antibodies**, which we will discuss in more detail a little later on, often attach themselves onto the surface of the invaders. This helps the phagocytes to recognize and attack the micro-organisms. These antibodies are produced by another kind of white blood cell known as a **lymphocyte** <LIM-fo-site>. Along with antibodies that are attached to the surface of the invader, antibodies circulating in the bloodstream also help to fight infections.

The type of lymphocyte that produces antibodies is known as a B cell. Once a B cell becomes activated, it changes into a plasma cell. The antibodies produced by this cell will neutralize chemicals known as **antigens** that are produced by the invading microorganisms. In addition, the surface proteins of bacteria, viruses, fungi, and other microorganisms can act as antigens because they are foreign to the body.

When a person comes down with a particular disease, such as poliomyelitis, the proteins on the surface of the virus are recognized by the immune system as foreign. The B cells are activated by the presence of the antigens (a process known as sensitization), convert to plasma cells, and produce antibodies that recognize the surface proteins of the virus. Once the B cell is sensitized, it may change to a plasma cell only when it gets a signal from another type of lymphocyte. This lymphocyte is called a helper T cell. Without the "OK" from the helper T cell, no antibodies will be produced.

Figure 3.2 White blood cells act as the body's soldiers to protect it from harm. The phagocyte is one of these soldiers. When a phagocyte encounters a foreign particle, it will engulf the particle through a process call phagocytosis. The phagocyte reaches out "arms" which will surround the particle and pull it inside the phagocyte, as can be seen in the diagram above.

When the B cells are introduced for the first time to the foreign antigens of the poliovirus, it will take some time for the body to produce the necessary antibodies to fight the invading organisms. This is known as the primary response. Unfortunately, during the time needed to produce the antibodies, the virus can incubate and cause disease. Vaccinations initiate a low level response by introducing a small amount of the antigen into the body. This is not enough to cause the disease, but rather to stimulate the body to produce antibodies. Thus, the need for vaccinations is of utmost importance.

Once a primary response occurs, the B cells are able to memorize the structure of the antigen for future reference. Should the body be exposed again to the same antigen, the B cells can swiftly make antibodies long before the organism has a chance to cause the disease. This antibody production caused by re-exposure to the antigen is called the secondary response. It is also known as the **anamnestic** <ann-am-NESS-tick> response. This is where the vaccine enters the picture.

THE FIRST VACCINE

The concept behind the first vaccine was actually very simple. A method was needed to expose a person to a disease, have them make protective antibodies, and be sure they did not actually develop the disease. Of course, the concept may have been simple, but the difficult part was how to go about doing the work.

During the Sung Dynasty in China (A.D. 960–1280), the Chinese people routinely practiced a procedure known as *variolation* in order to protect against smallpox. A person would place the powdered crusts of smallpox pustules into a scratch or inhale the dust. In most cases, the individual would develop a mild form of the disease and then become immune to smallpox for life. Unfortunately, some people would develop a true case of smallpox and die. However, this did not happen very often, so people were willing to undergo the procedure in order to be protected against the deadly disease.

Variolation continued to be used in China and the Middle East during this period but did not appear in Europe until the early 1700s. When Lady Mary Wortley Montagu, the wife of the British ambassador to Turkey, immunized her children against smallpox using this method, it became popular in Europe. Unfortunately, people who underwent this procedure were contagious. In addition, the procedure was expensive and only the rich could afford to be variolated. These factors left most of the population unprotected.

Later, in 1796, the first vaccine that would eventually be recognized as safe was administered. At that time, a British physician named Edward Jenner wondered why milkmaids who had developed cowpox (a disease similar to smallpox but not as life-threatening) did not develop smallpox. During this period in history, as in the past, smallpox was recognized as one of the worst diseases known to man. It often killed its victims, many of whom were infants and children.

As an intelligent physician, Jenner compared the pox found on cows that had cowpox to those on humans with smallpox. He realized that there was a great similarity between the two diseases and concluded that the milkmaids must have developed resistance to smallpox from their exposure to cowpox, which was a much milder disease.

A DANGEROUS EXPERIMENT

In order to test his theory, Jenner performed a daring and dangerous experiment. On May 14, 1796, a milkmaid by the name of Sara Nelmes came to Jenner suffering from a case of cowpox. Jenner took a piece of metal, scratched several of her pox with it, and then transferred the material he had

Figure 3.3 In a daring experiment, Edward Jenner deliberately exposed James Phipps to cowpox. After the boy recovered from the disease, which is a more mild form of the disease smallpox, he was shown to be immune to smallpox. This painting depicts Jenner inoculating the boy with material from a pustule of milkmaid Sara Nelmes, who had cowpox. Jenner's experiment paved the way for vaccine research.

collected to James Phipps, his gardener's son (Figure 3.3). James soon developed cowpox.

On July 1, once James had recovered from cowpox, Jenner attempted to give him a case of smallpox. When James did not develop the disease, Jenner declared that the boy was successfully vaccinated. The word "vaccination" was derived from the Latin word *vacca*, meaning cow.

In 1798, following his success, Jenner published his findings in a book entitled *An Inquiry into the Causes and Effects of the Variolæ Vaccinæ*. He spent the rest of his career studying the vaccination process, promoting it, and supplying physicians with cowpox material so that they could also vaccinate people against smallpox. He summed up his dedication to the cause by saying, "I shall myself continue to prosecute this inquiry, encouraged by the pleasing hope of its becoming essentially beneficial to mankind."

Today, there are many vaccines available to help protect us from diseases that were once devastating to mankind. They are delivered either by injection or by mouth, as is done with the Sabin vaccine against poliomyelitis. In the end, they all work in the same way. Their purpose is to stimulate the immune system to produce antibodies and to keep a memory of the foreign invader or toxin that will cause a disease. With this memory, if the body is exposed to the real disease organisms or toxins, an immediate production of antibodies will take place and protect us.

MAKING THE VACCINE

In order to make the vaccine, the organism (such as the poliovirus) or a toxin made by an organism (such as that seen in a case of **tetanus**) must be either weakened or destroyed, a process called *attenuation.* One way this can be done is by cooling the tissue culture in which the virus is grown, thus creating a virus that grows slowly at body temperature. The organism can also be treated with special chemicals, such as aluminum salts when we want to make a tetanus **toxoid** vaccine, or **formaldehyde** <form-AL-de-hide> for making other vaccines.

Two scientists, Jonas Salk and Albert Sabin, worked independently to create a polio vaccine. The Salk polio vaccine was created by killing the virus with formaldehyde and then purifying the mixture to collect the dead virus. Sabin used a live, **attenuated** <a-TEN-u-ate-ed>, or weakened, virus in his vaccine. In this type of vaccine, the virus is grown in culture at lower than normal temperatures. Over time, a strain of virus that can exist at these lower temperatures develops. When purified and collected, the virus can infect human cells, but only very slowly because it is now used to growing at colder than body temperature. The slow development of the virus in the vaccinated individual allows the immune system to create antibodies before a true case of the disease can make the person ill. This technique is also used to create the measles vaccine. The work of Salk and Sabin will be described in more detail in Chapters 4 and 5.

Another type of vaccine is called the **subunit vaccine**. This is made by isolating the antigens or parts of the antigens of the infectious organism and introducing these to the patient. Today, vaccines made in this way are used to fight against meningitis, pneumonia, whooping cough (also known as pertussis <per-TUSS-iss>), and a serious childhood respiratory disease caused by the bacterium *Haemophilus influenzae* type b.

DID YOU KNOW THAT . . .

In light of the recent attention to **bioterrorism**, many people have voiced concerns about the possibility that terrorists might use the smallpox virus as a weapon. Because smallpox as a disease has been eradicated from the face of the earth, doctors have not been giving vaccinations for many years. The government of the United States has assured its people that there is sufficient smallpox vaccine in storage to vaccinate the entire population of the United States, if necessary.

Modern technological advances have led to the development of recombinant vaccines. These are made by taking the actual genes for a part of the viral protein coat and putting them into yeast cells which then go on to produce the protein for the viral coat. The proteins are then injected into the patient thus causing antibody production. This is a safe means of vaccinating an individual because the protein contains no viral DNA or RNA and, therefore, cannot infect a cell. However, it will bring about the production of antibodies to the viral coat protein. In addition to this, genetically engineered bacteria have been used to create safe vaccines in experimental trials.

4

The Life of Jonas Salk

In New York City on October 28, 1914, a baby was born who would eventually change the condition of humanity forever. It was on this day that Jonas Edward Salk became the first child of Jewish-Russian immigrant parents. His father was a garment worker and his mother worked hard to make sure that her children received a good education and became successful (Figure 4.1).

Salk was the first in his family to attend college. While at the City University of New York, his initial desire was to become a lawyer. In fact, as a child he was not interested in the sciences. After a short time in college, however, his interests changed and he decided to pursue a career in medicine. Salk has said that part of this change in careers might have been due to his mother. "My mother didn't think I would make a very good lawyer. And I believe that her reasons were that I really couldn't win an argument with her."

A RESEARCH CAREER BEGINS

Following college, he entered New York University School of Medicine. At the end of his first year, he was asked to meet with the professor of chemistry, Dr. R. Keith Cannon. Salk was sure that he would be told he was failing or had done something wrong. Instead, Dr. Cannon offered him the opportunity to postpone medical school for one year and conduct chemistry research. Salk had always wanted to do research, so he took Cannon up on his offer.

Jonas Salk graduated from medical school in 1938. At that time, he began to work with a **microbiologist** named Thomas Francis, Jr. Together, they worked on creating a vaccine for **influenza**. This

Figure 4.1 Jonas Salk, inventor of the first polio vaccine, examines test tubes in his laboratory at the University of Pittsburgh. After eight years of research, he created a vaccine using an inactivated form of the polio virus. The vaccine was given to the public beginning April 12, 1955.

dreaded disease had killed millions of people during World War I, and scientists hoped to find a vaccine to avoid another devastating outbreak. Salk and Francis were successful and created a vaccine in 1942 that was used by armed forces personnel during World War II.

In 1947, Salk began research at the University of Pittsburgh Medical School. The National Foundation for Infantile Paralysis, aware of his success with the influenza vaccine, wanted him to work with them on a vaccine for polio. He spent the next eight years in an effort to create such a vaccine. His dedication to his work may easily be seen in the following quotation during a 1991 interview in San Diego, California:

> We were told in one lecture that it was possible to immunize against diphtheria and tetanus by the use of chemically treated toxins, or toxoids. And the following lecture, we were told that for immunization against a virus disease, you have to experience the infection, and that you could not induce immunity with the so-called "killed" or inactivated, chemically treated virus preparation. Well, somehow, that struck me. What struck me was that both statements couldn't be true. And I asked why this was so, and the answer that was given was in a sense, "Because." There was no satisfactory answer.[5]

DID YOU KNOW THAT . . .

Although the Salk vaccine was a huge success, initially there was a problem with the vaccine. The vaccine actually induced 260 cases of poliomyelitis, including ten deaths. The problem was traced to incomplete inactivation of some virus particles, which was soon corrected. Since then the vaccine has been highly effective, with a 70–90 percent protection rate.[6]

5. Interview with Jonas Salk, May 16, 1991, San Diego.
   http://www.achievement.org/autodoc/page/sal0bio-1

6. Maybury Okonek, Bonnie A. and Linda Morganstein, (editors). *Development of Polio Vaccines.* Washington, DC: The National Health Museum, 2002.
   http://www.accessexcellence.org/AE/AEC/CC/polio.html

Surely, Salk was a man who did not believe in following others. He was always thinking, challenging, and creating. Hard work did not daunt him.

During the same interview, Salk said that he was curious, even as a young child.

> There was a photograph of me when I was a year old, and there was that look of curiosity on that infant's face that is inescapable. I have the suspicion that this curiosity was very much a part of my early life: asking questions about unreasonableness. I tended to observe, and reflect and wonder. That sense of wonder, I think, is built into us.

SWEET SUCCESS

On July 2, 1952, Salk used a refined vaccine on children who had already suffered from a case of polio and recovered. Once vaccinated, the antibody levels in their blood increased. Following this, he tried his vaccine on volunteers who had never been exposed to polio. This included his wife, children, and himself. Once again, antibodies were produced and nobody became ill.

This was very encouraging to Salk. In fact, he would later say that the experience was, "the thrill of my life. Compared to the feeling I got looking under the microscope, everything that followed was anticlimactic." The governmental leaders were also very proud and wanted the world to know that Salk's success was achieved in Pittsburgh. Much publicity followed in an effort to show that the city was a major center of medical care and research.

In 1955, after much hard work and dedication, Jonas Salk was successful in releasing the first vaccine effective against the dreaded poliovirus (Figure 4.2). On April 12, 1955, news of the creation of the vaccine was released to the public. Millions breathed a sigh of relief in the knowledge that finally, one of the great scourges of mankind would be defeated. In addition to this, Salk was hailed as a hero, not only for his success, but also because he refused to patent his discovery. He did not care whether or not he would become rich from it, he merely wanted the vaccine to be available to as many people as possible.

Salk made his vaccine from "killed" virus that he treated with formaldehyde. The treatment rendered the virus completely unable to cause polio. This is in contrast to Albert Sabin's technique (see Chapter 4), which used a weakened, or attenuated, virus that could still cause polio in someone with a weakened immune system.

Although the virus was no longer able to cause a case of polio, it was still capable of bringing about an immune response that would protect an individual if he or she were exposed to the live virus.

THE SALK INSTITUTE OPENS

In 1963, Salk opened the Jonas Salk Institute for Biological Studies in La Jolla, California. The National Science Foundation and the March of Dimes were instrumental in the funding of the research center. Salk's problem had been in deciding where to open the institute. In 1960, Charles Dail, the mayor of San Diego, offered Salk 70 acres of land right next to the University of California at San Diego. He took the offer and the rest was history. Incidentally, Mayor Dail was himself a victim of polio.

After his phenomenal success with the polio vaccine, Salk did not rest (Figure 4.3). He spent several years writing. He released *Man Unfolding* in 1972, a book that focused on the pattern of order in living things. In 1973, he published *The Survival of the Wisest,* which stressed that man will survive if he makes judgments in advance rather than after he has acted on something. Salk went on to publish *World Population and Human Values: A New Reality* in 1981. This book looked at the

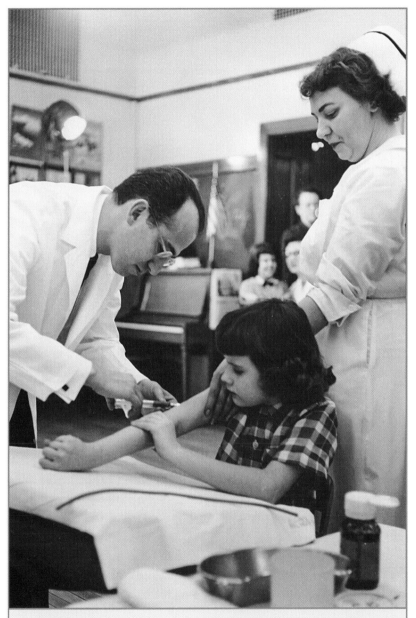

Figure 4.2 In this 1954 photo, Jonas Salk administers his polio vaccine to a young girl. The polio vaccine went through extensive field testing before it was released to the general public in 1955.

Figure 4.3 In 1963, Jonas Salk opened the Salk Institute, located in La Jolla, California. The Institute was funded by the National Science Foundation and the March of Dimes. The mayor of San Diego at that time, a polio victim himself, offered Salk the land on which the Institute resides.

changing values of society as the world population increased. In 1983 he wrote *Anatomy of Reality* in which he stated, "The most meaningful activity in which a human being can be engaged is one that is directly related to human evolution."

His last years were devoted to work on finding a vaccine for the world's new dreaded disease, AIDS. Unfortunately, he never succeeded as he had with his polio vaccine. Jonas Salk died of congestive heart failure on June 23, 1995. His legacy will live on forever.

5

The Life of Albert Sabin

On the summer day of August 26, 1906, in Bialystok, Poland, Tillie and Jacob Sabin became the proud parents of a son named Albert. He grew up as one of four children in his native land until 1921 when, due to the spread of anti-Semitism, his parents decided it would be wise to immigrate to the United States.

The family settled in Paterson, New Jersey, and his father entered the silk and manufacturing business. Albert spoke no English, but he learned quickly. Two years after arriving in the United States, Albert entered New York University. In 1924, only one year after his admission, he earned a bachelor of arts degree. He continued his education until 1926 at the NYU College of Dentistry. He received his bachelor of science degree in 1927.

Sabin was clearly a brilliant student. He furthered his studies by entering the NYU Medical College in 1927 (the same college from which Jonas Salk graduated) and graduated in 1931. He went on to become the house physician at Bellevue Hospital in New York. Then, in 1934, he received a National Research Council fellowship at the Lister Institute in London, England.

Sabin continued his work in London for only one year. He returned to New York to work as a research assistant at the prestigious Rockefeller Institute for Medical Research. His research interests at the institute included work with viruses and the immune system. He had success in cultivating the rabies virus in the laboratory and creating a better rabies vaccine for dogs. He also worked with pneumonia and polio.

Albert Sabin was responsible for discovering the true nature of the poliovirus (Figure 5.1). Originally, it was believed that the virus was a

Figure 5.1 Albert Sabin created the oral version of the polio vaccine. The oral vaccine had several advantages over the Salk vaccine, including ease of administration. In this photo, Sabin examines cell cultures in his laboratory.

member of the herpesvirus family. Sabin proved that it was a newly discovered virus in a family not previously identified. He also showed how poliovirus entered the body. It had been believed that the mode of entry was through the nasal membranes. Sabin showed that the virus entered more often through the digestive system.

In 1939, Sabin became an associate professor at the Children's Hospital Research Foundation at the University of Cincinnati in Ohio. Thanks to his efforts, a Department of Virology and Microbiology was established there.

Sabin served in the United States Army during World War II. He worked for the Army's Board for the Investigation of Epidemic Diseases. While there, he focused his research on sandfly fever virus and dengue virus. After World War II he concentrated his efforts on polio research.

IN SEARCH OF A WEAK VIRUS

While reviewing data on the incidence of polio outbreaks, Sabin noticed that cases of polio were rare in areas of poor sanitation. Studies of antibody presence in children who lived in these areas showed that most of the children did, indeed, have antibodies to polio, but had never shown any symptoms of the disease. Sabin believed that these children had either been exposed to polio very early in life, when they still had antibodies from their mothers, or had been infected by weak strains of the virus that caused the production of antibodies without any symptoms.

Sabin began a quest to locate these weak viruses and traveled around the world in an effort to do so. He found three strains and began his work on an oral polio vaccine. The most frequently occurring strain of poliovirus is Strain I, also known as "Brunhilde." The other strains are Strain II (Lansing) and Strain III (Leon). Sabin intended for the vaccine to be delivered orally in a syrup form or on a sugar cube. The process by which he made the vaccine was described in Chapter 3.

EUREKA!

After much work and dedication, Sabin met with success. The World Health Organization (WHO) felt so confident that the vaccine was effective, it ordered testing on a worldwide basis. In 1954, Sabin tested the vaccine on himself and his two daughters. In 1957, Sabin was invited to be involved with the administration of the vaccine in Mexico, Chile, Sweden, Japan, Holland, and Russia. Sabin, just as Salk, did not patent his vaccine and did not profit from its discovery.

Unfortunately, Sabin's success did not meet with the same acceptance in the United States as in other countries. Although an oral vaccine using attenuated virus would be more effective than an injected vaccine using killed virus, scientists believed that there was no better vaccine than the one developed by Jonas Salk. Testing and acceptance of Sabin's vaccine was delayed.

Sabin's oral vaccine had definite advantages over Salk's. The most obvious was that it did not require an injection (Figure 5.2). Children were much less afraid of taking the vaccine. Secondly, because Sabin's vaccine used live attenuated, or weakened, virus instead of the killed virus used by Salk, it brought about immunity in the intestinal tract where the virus first established itself. This would cause the destruction of the virus at the site of infection and not allow the virus to be spread through fecal contamination. Bodily immunity also developed from this mode of viral introduction.

The Salk vaccine, because it was injected, did not expose intestinal cells to the virus, and only bodily immunity was created. This meant that, although a person vaccinated with the Salk vaccine was protected against polio, he or she could still be a **carrier** of the disease in their intestinal tract if they were exposed to a wild form of the virus.

Another benefit of Sabin's vaccine was that no booster vaccination was needed. With Salk's vaccine, several booster injections had to be administered in order for a person to develop full immunity to the virus. This meant less time spent by the patient and by the physician. The cost was lower as well.

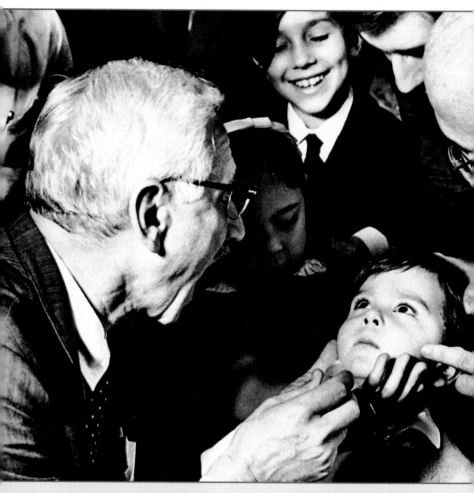

Figure 5.2 Albert Sabin first tested his polio vaccine on himself and his two daughters. Sabin is pictured here asking five-year-old Luiz Inacio Gama to open his mouth so that he can administer the vaccine.

SABIN SUNDAY

On April 24, 1960, the first test of Sabin's vaccine was held in the United States. Approximately 200,000 people lined up at numerous locations to receive vaccine. The day was referred to as "Sabin Sunday" and was a momentous occasion for the new vaccine and its creator (Figure 5.3). It was followed by two more "Sabin Sundays." By this time, 80 million people throughout the world had already been vaccinated. In 1970, Sabin received the National Medal of Science from President Richard Nixon. The president awarded the medal ". . . for the vaccine that has eliminated poliomyelitis as a major threat to human health."

That same year, Sabin left Cincinnati to settle in Israel where he became the president of the Weizmann Institute of Science. He remained in that position for two years before he

DID YOU KNOW THAT . . .

The World Health Organization has been keeping a close watch on the occurrence of polio cases worldwide. Here a map showing where the "hotspots" have been located from 1988 through 2000.

Progress towards poliomyelitis eradication, 1988 – end of 2000.

350,000 cases in 1988

*Estimated by WHO as of 3 April 2001

Less than 3,500 cases in 2000*

Figure 5.3 The Sabin oral polio vaccine was quite a success. On the first day the vaccine was offered, 200,000 people chose to receive it. Due to the large turnout, the day was called "Sabin Sunday." In the 1961 photo above, people line up at a Georgia grocery store to receive the vaccine.

had to step down to undergo open-heart surgery. After his recovery, he dedicated himself to research on cancer and a spray vaccine for measles.

In the early 1980s, Sabin was stricken with a disease that caused temporary paralysis. The condition, known as Guillain-Barré <ge-EN-bar-A> syndrome, is not related to polio in any way. It is usually the result of recovering from the flu or other respiratory illnesses and is often not a permanent problem. Following his recovery, Sabin became the senior consultant to the AIDS researchers at the National Institutes of Health in Bethesda, Maryland.

Figure 5.4 Albert Sabin received the Presidential Medal of Freedom in 1986 for his work with the polio vaccine. His vaccine has helped to eradicate polio in the United States and is used in other countries as well. He is pictured here in his laboratory at the University of Cincinnati College of Medicine.

THE PRESIDENTIAL MEDAL OF FREEDOM

On May 12, 1986, Sabin received the Presidential Medal of Freedom from President Ronald Reagan. This is the highest award given to a civilian. In that same year, the city of Cincinnati renamed its newly expanded convention center after Albert Sabin (Figure 5.4).

THE PRESIDENTIAL MEDAL OF FREEDOM

The following is a partial transcript of the ceremony on May 12, 1986, when Albert Sabin, along with six other individuals, received the Presidential Medal of Freedom from President Ronald Reagan. The following is a portion of the President's speech:

Well, thank you all for being here. Nancy and I want to welcome you all to the White House for this happy occasion. On days like this and at lunches like this, I find myself looking up and thinking what a wonderful job I have. We're here today to present the Medal of Freedom to seven Americans. This medal is the highest civilian honor our nation can bestow. And I've always thought it highly significant that we call it not the Medal of Talent or the Medal of Valor or the Medal of Courage or Genius but the Medal of Freedom. I think that says a lot about our values and what we honor and what we love.

. . . You're all originals. You've all made America better—a better place—and you've made it seem a better place in the eyes of the people of the world. And this today is just our way of saying thanks. And without further ado, I'm going to read the citations for the medals now and award them to the recipients.

. . . When, as a boy, Albert Bruce Sabin came to the United States from Russia, no one could have known that he would number among the most prominent immigrants of our century. From an early age Sabin devoted his life to medicine, and by the 1950's his research had resulted in a breakthrough. In the years since the Sabin vaccine has helped to make dramatic advances against the scourge of poliomyelitis.

This medal is awarded to Dr. Sabin on behalf of a proud nation and a grateful world. Doctor, thank you for everything.

There's nothing to add to achievements such as these, and no praise that can add any more luster to these great names. May I say to you simply, to all of you, thank you just for being, for doing what you've done and what you do. And thank you all, and God bless you.[7]

---

7. Remarks at the Presentation Ceremony for the Presidential Medal of Freedom, May 12, 1986.
   http://www.reagan.utexas.edu/resource/speeches/1986/51286b.htm

Albert Sabin died in 1993 at the age of 86. It was estimated, at that time, that his vaccine had prevented nearly five million cases of polio. In addition, it probably helped 500,000 people worldwide avoid death from the once dreaded disease.

6

Nobody is Exempt

Viruses and bacteria are usually not picky about what type of people they infect. They do not care, for example, whether a person is rich or poor. No matter what walk of life a person comes from, he or she is still quite able to catch any number of diseases and possibly die from them.

This has been the case with polio. Many rich and famous people were unable to escape it. Consider Franklin Delano Roosevelt. His experience with the disease was explained in Chapter 2. He may have gone on to become a president, but his life was permanently changed by polio.

Many other famous people, both men and women, have been stricken with polio. Some of these were athletes, some actors, and others musicians. They often contracted the disease in their childhood, and in some cases it left a lasting mark. However, the consequences of the disease did not stop them from achieving what they set out to do.

ALAN ALDA

On January 28, 1936, Alphonso D'Abruzzo was born in New York City to Robert Alda and Joan Brown. Robert was an actor and Joan was a former Miss New York pageant winner. In 1943, at the age of seven, Alphonso, later to be known as the famous actor Alan Alda (Figure 6.1), developed polio. He was confined to his bed for two years.

Thanks to his mother's efforts and her knowledge of the work of Sister Elizabeth Kenny, Alan was able to overcome his disease with no lasting problems. His mother used Kenny's technique of bandaging, massaging, and applying hot packs to his legs. He did

Figure 6.1 Many famous people have suffered from polio. Alan Alda, who starred in the hit television series *M*A*S*H*, suffered from the debilitating disease. Although he was confined to his bed for two years as a young boy, his mother used the techniques pioneered by Sister Kenny, and Alda fully recovered.

not forget his two years of therapy, as can be seen by the passage below:

> The massages were extremely painful. It was a little bit like taking your thumb and bending it back to your elbow. To this day I'm not interested in getting a massage. People think it's wonderful. Not me. It's torture."[8]

---

8. Byrne, Bridget. "Alan Alda Smoothly Shifts Gears." *SouthCoast Today.* *http://www.s-t.com/daily/04-01/04-08-01/e06li150.htm*

Nevertheless, Alda was able to develop normally and went on to become one of the most famous television and movie actors today. His list of television and theatrical movies is long and impressive. Of course, his most famous role is probably that of Captain Benjamin Franklin "Hawkeye" Pierce on the television series *M*A*S*H.*

EMPEROR CLAUDIUS

Another famous person who suffered from polio lived in a different period of history, in a different land, and under very different circumstances. Claudius, Emperor of Rome, lived from 10 B.C. to A.D. 54. He was born Tiberius Claudius Drusus to emperor Drusus Claudius Nero and his wife Antonia, who was the daughter of Mark Antony.

Claudius suffered from a very serious limp due to what was probably polio and was constantly ill. Because he was eventually supposed to ascend the throne of Rome and was clearly disabled, he was kept out of sight for most of his childhood. Because of his disabilities, his parents considered him to be mentally infirm and therefore an embarrassment. Claudius spent most of his childhood in complete seclusion. However, he was not the unintelligent person that his family assumed him to be. Because he had a lot of free time on his hands, he read many books and became very knowledgeable. It was not until he was 46 years old that he held his first public office as a consul.

Through a series of events that included assassinations and overthrows, Claudius became Emperor of Rome on January 25, A.D. 41. His polio did not shorten his lifespan. Unfortunately, he was assassinated on October 13, A.D. 54.

WILMA RUDOLPH

Who could have ever imagined that a young girl who suffered from polio would one day become an Olympic medal winner for track and field? Despite her illness, Wilma Rudolph achieved this goal (Figure 6.2).

Figure 6.2 Wilma Rudolph contracted polio at the age of six and had to wear leg braces to help her walk. That did not stop her from being active. She was finally able to walk without braces and, at the age of 16, won the bronze medal at the 1960 Summer Olympics in Rome, Italy (pictured above).

Wilma was born in Tennessee on June 23, 1940, to Ed and Blanche Rudolph, poor but honest, hard-working people. She was the twentieth of 22 children. Wilma was born prematurely and weighed only four and one-half pounds. Because the family was poor, they could not afford good health care. In addition, due to the segregation in the South, she was not allowed to be treated in the local, whites only hospital. So her mother treated her at home for several illnesses including scarlet fever and pneumonia.

When Wilma was six, her mother noticed that her left leg and foot were becoming deformed. When doctors examined her, they told her mother that Wilma would never walk again. However, Blanche Rudolph was not one to give up easily. She found out that Wilma could be treated at Meharry Hospital, located about 50 miles away. They made the journey, and at the age of six, the doctors fitted Wilma with leg braces. "I spent most of my time trying to figure out how to get them off," she said. "But when you come from a large, wonderful family, there's always a way to achieve your goals."

With help and support from her entire family, Wilma was able to remove her leg braces by the age of nine. After this, she became an avid basketball player. She spent a good deal of time playing basketball and eventually found that she was an excellent runner.

In 1956, at the age of 16, she competed in her first Olympic games and won a bronze medal in the 4x4 relay. At the Rome Olympics, on September 7, 1960, she was the first American woman to win three gold medals. She won for the 100-meter dash, the 200-meter dash, and as the anchor in the 400-meter relay. In 1983, she was elected to the United States Olympic Hall of Fame.

After retiring from competition, Wilma became a track coach at Burt High School in Clarksville, Tennessee. Later she coached in Maine and Indiana and became a sports commentator on national television. On November 12, 1994, she died at the age of 54 of brain cancer at her home in Nashville, Tennessee.

ITZHAK PERLMAN

Born on August 31, 1945, in Tel-Aviv, Israel, Itzhak Perlman was unfortunate enough to contract polio at the young age of four. This caused him to permanently lose the use of his legs. But it did not stop him from becoming one of the most celebrated violinists in history. Although he is permanently disabled by

Figure 6.3 Itzhak Perlman (pictured above) cannot walk without crutches as a result of suffering from polio as a young boy. He has achieved excellence through music and is a world-renowned violinist. Although it takes him a long time to climb the stage for a performance, audiences wait patiently to hear him play.

his condition and must continue to use leg braces and crutches to get around, Mr. Perlman is known for being a jovial person. He has even appeared on Sesame Street and played for several of the characters as well as many children (Figure 6.3).

Perlman's dedication to his craft was described in an article that appeared in the Houston Chronicle. A description of how hard it is for him to negotiate the stage makes it clear just how much he loves his music and does not let polio interfere with his ability to perform.

DID YOU KNOW THAT . . .

Some famous people from all walks of life have suffered from polio. Here are just a few:

Ann Adams (1937–1992): artist, used her mouth to paint

Alan Alda: television star

Claudius: Emperor of Rome (10 B.C.–54 A.D.)

Arthur C. Clarke: author

Georgia Coleman (1912–1940): olympic diver

CeDell Davis: jazz guitarist

Ian Dury (1942–2000): British rock star

Ray Ewry (1873–1937): Olympic track and field champion

Mia Farrow: actress

Henry Holden: actor, comedian, athlete, activist

Marjorie Lawrence (1908–1979): world famous opera singer

Joni Mitchell: singer

Jack Nicklaus: golfer

Itzhak Perlman: internationally acclaimed violinist

Ruma: ancient Syrian

Siptah: Egyptian Pharaoh (lived 20 years around 1200 B.C.)

Franklin Delano Roosevelt (1882–1945): United States president

Wilma Rudolph (1940–1994): athlete, Olympic gold medalist

On Nov. 18, 1995, Itzhak Perlman, the violinist, came on stage to give a concert at Avery Fisher Hall at Lincoln Center in New York City. If you have ever been to a Perlman concert, you know that getting on stage is no small achievement for him. He was stricken with polio as a child, and so he has braces on both legs and walks with the aid of two crutches.

To see him walk across the stage one step at a time, painfully and slowly, is an unforgettable sight. He walks painfully, yet majestically, until he reaches his chair. Then he sits down, slowly, puts his crutches on the floor, undoes the clasps on his legs, tucks one foot back and extends the other foot forward. Then he bends down and picks up the violin, puts it under his chin, nods to the conductor and proceeds to play.

By now, the audience is used to this ritual. They sit quietly while he makes his way across the stage to his chair. They remain reverently silent while he undoes the clasps on his legs. They wait until he is ready to play."[8]

Perlman began his training at the Tel Aviv Schulamit Academy shortly after contracting polio. By the time he was ten years old, he was performing concerts with the Israel Broadcasting Orchestra. His family moved to New York where he attended the prestigious Julliard School of Music. In 1964, he won the highly acclaimed Leventritt Competition. This was the key that opened the door to a career that now includes hundreds of performances, recordings, television appearances, and awards.

In Itzhak Perlman's case, polio may have left him with a permanent disability that does not allow him to walk, but it surely did not stop him from achieving a level of success that most people only dream about.

---

8. Riemer, Jack. "Playing a Violin With Three Strings." *Houston Chronicle.* (February 10, 2001)

7

Just When We Thought it was Safe: Post-Polio Syndrome

Thanks to the creation of the Salk and Sabin vaccines, the number of polio cases has consistently decreased since the 1950s. However, in the late 1970s, symptoms began to appear in people who had recovered from paralytic polio years earlier. The symptoms included pain in muscles and joints, excessive fatigue, and increased muscle weakness.

The doctors had never seen anything like this, except when these people originally contracted polio. They had no name for the condition and no way to treat it. It had always been believed that with rehabilitation and therapy, most polio survivors would achieve a level of functioning that would remain the same for the rest of their lives. Now that belief was being turned upside down.

The number of cases of this strange **syndrome** kept increasing. When the data were studied, it was seen that the syndrome appeared ten to 40 years after the patient had suffered from the **acute** illness. The doctors were stumped.

THE SYNDROME GETS A NAME
With the ever-increasing frequency of the syndrome, it was finally given a name. In the early 1980s, the term post-polio syndrome (PPS) was coined. It was defined as a neurological disorder with a variety of symptoms that occurs in patients who recovered several years earlier from a case of

paralytic polio. The most serious symptom is a new case of progressive muscle weakness.

The actual cause of the symptoms is the death of individual motor nerve cells that remain alive in the spinal cord after the initial attack of polio. These cells had to take over the function of cells that were destroyed during the initial attack of the disease. In order to do this, they had to grow new branches so they could communicate with muscles that once received nerve impulses from the now destroyed nerve cells. This put a great strain on them and they were highly susceptible to being destroyed (Figure 7.1).

Motor nerve cells are responsible for transmitting the signal that comes down the spinal cord from the brain to nerves that go directly to muscles. The degree of severity of post-polio syndrome symptoms depends on how seriously the individual was affected by the actual case of polio in the first place and how many of these cells remained unaffected by the disease. Interestingly, it was found that PPS is brought about by some serious stress to the body. This could be a fall, a disease that caused the patient to need extended bed rest, an accident, or surgery.

HOW IS IT DIAGNOSED?

Post-polio syndrome is difficult to diagnose accurately. Part of the problem is making sure that the muscle weakness is progressive. In order to determine this, the patient must make repeated visits to the doctor so that a continuous decrease in muscle strength may be documented. Of course, neurological examinations and other laboratory tests must also be performed to rule out other neuromuscular diseases.

Another problem that doctors face is trying to be objective about the progress of the muscle weakness. This can be very difficult, as there is no specific machine that can accurately determine if a muscle, or group of muscles is getting weaker, or if the patient is just having a bad day. Doctors may use magnetic resonance imaging (MRI), neuroimaging, and

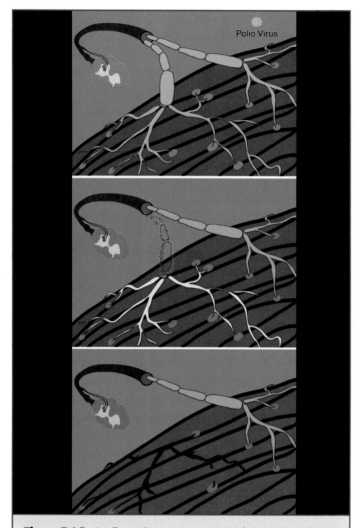

Figure 7.1 Post-polio syndrome causes progressive muscle weakness due to strain on the nerves that send signals to the muscles. When nerve cells die during an initial attack of polio, other nerve cells must take over the job of the dead cells. These new cells are working twice as hard as usual, and eventually may begin to degrade from the added strain. The top panel shows two branches of a nerve cell which help to control a muscle. In the middle panel, the branch on the left begins to degrade. In the bottom panel, the branch is completely dead and can no longer send signals to the muscle.

electrophysiological <e-LEK-tro-fizz-e-o-logic-el> studies to help make the diagnosis. These latter tests involve the use of needles placed into the muscle at different sites and the passage of an electric current through the muscle to determine its condition. In addition, a muscle **biopsy** may be performed. This test takes a sample of the tissue and looks at it under the microscope to see if the muscle is actually damaged.

Dr. Lauro Halstead, director of the post-polio syndrome program at the National Rehabilitation Hospital in Washington, D.C., describes the syndrome very clearly:

My own experience seems to be typical of both recovery from paralytic polio and the new development of post-polio syndrome. I contracted polio during the epidemic of 1954 while traveling in Europe after my freshman year in college. I was 18 years old. My six-month journey of recovery took me from iron lung to wheelchair to foot brace and then to no assistive device at all. At times, improvement in strength seemed to happen overnight. Although my right arm remained paralyzed, the rest of my body regained most of the strength and endurance I had before my illness. As a result, I thought of myself as

DID YOU KNOW THAT . . .

In a study performed in 2002 at Haukeland University Hospital in Bergen, Norway, researchers found that some patients who had been diagnosed with non-paralytic polio between 1950 and 1954 are now showing motor weakness and symptoms similar to those seen in post-polio syndrome. The symptoms are similar to those associated with neuromuscular damage as is seen in PPS.[9]

9. Rekand, T., B. Karlsen, N. Langeland, and A. J. Aarli . "Long-term follow-up of patients with nonparalytic poliomyelitis." *Archives of Physical Medicine and Rehabilitation.* 83(4) (2002 April) 533-7.

cured. I returned to college, learned to write with my left hand and even played intramural squash. On the morning of the third anniversary of the onset of my polio, I reached the summit of Mount Fuji in Japan after a climb of over 12,000 feet. As I watched the sun rise, I thought, 'Polio is behind me. I have finally conquered it.'

With the conquest of Mount Fuji fresh in my mind, I began to look for other mountains to climb. After college, I entered medical school. Internship and residency initiated yet another cycle of physically demanding years. In short, I got on with my life while polio receded ever further in my memory. Several years ago I began developing new weakness in my legs. As the weakness progressed over a period of months, I went from being a full-time walker who jogged up six flights of stairs for exercise to having to use a motorized scooter full-time at work.[10]

Although it took until the 1980s to give post-polio syndrome a name, the syndrome had previously been mentioned in a French medical journal. Unfortunately, when the syndrome appeared in large numbers in the twentieth century, nobody remembered the original reference. In fact, between 1875 and 1975 there were actually at least 35 references in as many medical journals.

In 1984, scientists held a conference at the Warm Springs Institute for Rehabilitation. This is the institute in Georgia that was started by Franklin Delano Roosevelt in 1926 to treat polio victims (Figure 7.2). He opened the clinic because he felt that swimming in warm water helped to strengthen weak muscles.

---

10. Halstead, Lauro (ed.). *Managing Post-Polio: A guide to Living Well With Post-Polio Syndrome.* (Falls Church, Va.: NRH Press and ABI Professional Publications, 1998)

Figure 7.2 In 1926, President Roosevelt founded the Warm Springs Institute for Rehabilitation in Georgia because he believed that warm water and swimming would help polio victims. In the picture above, President Roosevelt swims at the Institute. Several polio symposiums have also been held at this location.

In 1986, another meeting was held that led to much more research into and understanding of post-polio syndrome. It stimulated interest in learning more about the syndrome as well. Even the United States government became involved. The National Center for Health Statistics, a group that collects data on diseases from households in the United States, calculated that there were more than 640,000 people who survived paralytic polio. This insight helped doctors to estimate the magnitude of the problem. Some research studies have claimed that as many as 40 percent of paralytic polio survivors may have post-polio syndrome. If this is true, there may be up to

250,000 people in the United States who are currently suffering from the syndrome.

With such a high number of people who probably suffer from the syndrome, the obvious question is, "Is there a treatment or a cure?" Unfortunately, just as it was with polio, the answer is no. There are a few experimental drugs being tested that show some promise in treating the symptoms, but nothing can replace dead cells in the spinal cord. The only recommendation is based on common sense: eat well, get plenty of rest, have regularly scheduled physical examinations, and avoid seriously stressful situations.

WHAT ABOUT THE FUTURE?

Post-polio syndrome is known to progress slowly and is associated with periods of stability where no further progress occurs. In fact, eventually there is no change in the status of the patient and no further paralysis occurs. Because of this clinical picture, PPS is usually not life-threatening. Of course, there is also no return of the lost muscle function once it disappears.

One serious cause of concern occurs in those patients that have experienced damage to their respiratory muscles during a bout with polio. In these patients, any further weakening of respiratory muscles, as occurs in PPS, may cause serious problems in breathing. If the degree of weakness is great, the patient may die of respiratory failure.

THE FAMOUS SUFFER HERE TOO
Joni Mitchell

As with polio, several famous people who had the disease now suffer from post-polio syndrome. One of these is Joni Mitchell (Figure 7.3). She was born Roberta Joan Anderson on November 7, 1943, in Fort McLeod, Alberta, Canada. Joni is a well-known singer who has been performing for over 30 years. She was diagnosed with polio at the

Figure 7.3 Joni Mitchell (pictured above) suffers from post-polio syndrome. She has experienced muscle weakness in her back, which made it difficult for her to hold her guitar. She has coped with the pain and discomfort by having a guitar specially designed so that it matches the contours of her body and places less stress on her back muscles.

age of nine. Then, in the 1980s, she was diagnosed with post-polio syndrome.

When interviewed on September 9, 1998, Joni described how she is dealing with PPS:

> . . . the 80s were a rough decade for me and on top of it I was diagnosed as having post-polio syndrome which they said was inevitable for I'm a polio survivor, that forty years after you had the disease, which is a disease of the

nervous system, the wires that animate certain muscles are taken out by the disease, and the body in its ingenious way, the filaments of the adjacent muscles send out branches and try to animate that muscle. It's kind of like the EverReady bunny, the muscles all around the muscles that are gone begin to go also because they've been trying to drive this muscle for so long. That's the nature of what was happening so I had it mostly in my back, so you don't see it as much as you would in a withered leg or an arm. But the weight of the guitar became unbearable. Also, acoustic guitar requires that you extend your shoulder out in an abnormal way and coincidentally some of the damage to my back in combination with that position was very painful. So, there was a merchant in Los Angeles who knew of my difficulties and knew that this machine was coming along that would solve my tuning problems and he made on spec a Stratocaster for me out of yellow cedar that was very light and thin as a wafer, so an electric guitar is a more comfortable design for my handicap. Then, a genius lothier built me this two and a half pound guitar which is not only beautiful to look at but it kind of contours to my body. It fits my hip and even kind of cups up like a bra! It's just beautifully designed and then also I abandoned regular medicine and fell into the hands first of a Kahuna and then a Chinese mystic acupuncturist who put down his pins and just points at you. I know this sounds real quacky but they did some mysterious good to the problem and I feel fine."[11]

It is encouraging to hear someone with post-polio syndrome explain how they are able to function well although

---

11. Interview with Joni Mitchell, conducted on September 9, 1998 by Jody Denberg that aired on KGSR-FM, Los Angeles, CA. *http://www.jonimitchell.com/JoniAndJodyIV98.html*

Figure 7.4 Science fiction author Arthur C. Clarke (*2001: A Space Odyssey*) also suffers from post-polio syndrome 45 years after he initially contracted the disease. He can no longer walk and must use a wheelchair to get around. However, he continues to write and persues an active lifestyle, including playing table tennis.

they have such a debilitating condition. Even with PPS, Ms. Mitchell has continued to perform and travel extensively.

Sir Arthur C. Clarke

Futurist, science fiction writer, and Renaissance man, Sir Arthur C. Clarke (Figure 7.4) was born in Minehead, Somerset, England on December 16, 1917. He became a prolific writer of science fiction stories and articles relating to various topics in the field of science.

In 1956, Clarke settled in Sri Lanka. In 1959, he contracted polio, but that did not stop him from continuing to write and lecture. In 1968, one of his most famous novels, *2001: A Space Odyssey*, was made into a very successful movie. Over the past few years he has suffered from post-polio syndrome and is confined to a wheelchair. Nevertheless, he is still very active in many areas including writing, observing the skies with a 14-inch telescope, playing table tennis, working with computers, and coming up with more futuristic ideas.

HOW TO DEAL WITH THE PAIN

For the many people who are suffering from post-polio syndrome, pain is a constant companion. The post-polio Research Group of Southeastern Wisconsin has a list of recommendations to help patients cope with PPS: [12]

1. Moist heat applied to the painful area.

2. Light massage to the painful area.

3. Ice packs applied to the painful area.

4. Chiropractic or osteopathic "adjustment" of neck/back/joints; postural improvement.

5. Alternative therapies such as acupuncture or electro-acupuncture to the ear lobe; magnetic field therapy.

6. Dietary supplements such as ginger, pycnogenol, cayenne pepper, glucosamine and chondroitin sulfates, calcium, and magnesium.

7. Treatment of sleeping difficulties, i.e., insufficient amount of deep, Stage IV (REM) sleep.

8. Treatment of breathing difficulties, i.e., insufficient amount of oxygen and or too much carbon dioxide, especially during sleep.

---

12. Post-Polio Research Group of Southeastern Wisconsin
   http://www.geocities.com/HotSprings/4760/pprg.html

9. Use of assistive and adaptive aids, as necessary, to reduce stress and strain to muscles and joints; assuring that all body parts that require it, e.g., neck, head, back, shoulders, are properly supported at all times.

10. For inflammation of muscles/joints—use of arthritis-type drugs: NSAIDs (Non-Steroidal Anti-Inflammatory Drugs). Over-the-counter types like aspirin, Ketoprofen, or prescription types like Relafen, Voltaren, Naprosyn.

11. For "nerve" pain—use of antidepressant prescription drugs—Elavil (amitriptyline)—an anti-depressant of the tricyclic type—is the first choice in drug therapy by some PPS specialist doctors for those with PPS pain AND trouble sleeping, at dosages less than would be used for clinical depression. But a lot of us don't tolerate it well. And for those who don't tolerate it (and also those who DON'T have sleeping problems), one of the SRUB class of anti-depressants (Serotonin ReUptake Blockers) such as Zoloft or Paxil—also in smaller doses than would be used for clinical depression—may be of help.

12. Occasional and/or careful use of muscle relaxants such as Quinine or Methocarbamol.

13. Hormone Replacement Therapy, especially for post-menopausal, post-hysterectomy women and others with lower than normal levels of estrogen, testosterone, thyroid, DHEA and precursors; Melatonin.

Will these recommendations work for all patients? Unfortunately not, but by using one or more of these approaches to treatment, a good percentage of those who are suffering from post-polio syndrome will find some degree of relief.

8

What Lies Ahead?
The Future of Polio

MAKING A VIRUS

If you needed to build a radio, you might go online and find a supplier or two that could provide you with the necessary parts. At some other website, you could probably even find the directions to do the work. It seems like a pretty simple concept. Who could ever imagine being able to go online and find the recipe to assemble a virus? Furthermore, who would think that the gene sequences needed would also be available from a mail-order supplier?

It may be mind-boggling, but this is exactly what was announced on July 11, 2002, when Dr. Eckard Wimmer (Figure 8.1), a professor in the Department of Molecular Genetics at the State University of New York at Stony Brook, and his team announced that they had created an infectious virus in a test tube. The virus could successfully infect living cells. The virus was poliovirus.

Although much of the world's population today is concerned with bioterrorism, according to Dr. Wimmer the technique may be used for good purposes. He suggested that scientists might be able to create and prepare vaccines at a much faster rate than before and also perform gene therapy. In addition, biological attacks may be more easily avoided thanks to this new technique.

Dr. Wimmer is no stranger to the poliovirus. He has been conducting research on the virus for many years. He has also worked with other viruses, studying their methods for reproduction, which is referred to as replication. Dr. Wimmer explained that he was able to purchase

Figure 8.1 Using new DNA technologies, viruses can be created in the laboratory. Dr. Eckard Wimmer (pictured above) of the University of New York at Stony Brook, created a version of the poliovirus in a test tube. He believes that his extensive virus research will help scientists to create better vaccines.

ready-made pieces of DNA from commercial sources. DNA is the genetic code that is found in all living creatures, from viruses right up to mankind itself (Figure 8.2). The letters

Figure 8.2 <u>D</u>eoxyribo<u>n</u>ucleic <u>A</u>cid (DNA) is the genetic code found in all living organisms. DNA directs all processes of life, from what an organism looks like to how it functions. The model in the picture above displays the double helix form of DNA.

stand for <u>D</u>eoxyribo<u>n</u>ucleic <u>A</u>cid. It directs all of our heredity and how a virus affects a living cell. The DNA sequence information of many disease-causing organisms is available on the web and may be used by any scientist who has the right knowledge, equipment, and money.

A DNA *sequence* is the order of the base pairs that make up DNA. Four different chemicals, arranged in precisely the correct order in a variety of ways, make up our genes. Once a researcher knows the correct order for a particular virus, he or she may string the genes together and make the virus work.

WORLDWIDE ERADICATION

As mentioned earlier, thanks to the development of the Salk and Sabin vaccines, the occurrence of polio worldwide has diminished considerably. The World Health Organization had established a goal of worldwide polio eradication by the year 2000. Unfortunately, that year has come and gone, and polio still exists, although in small numbers.

India is one of the places where the disease is still prevalent. In 1995, the Indian government improved its vaccine program to include biannual National Immunization Days designed to vaccinate young children. This was done in an effort to meet the goals set by the WHO. More than 79 million children were vaccinated under this program in 1995 and another 134 million in 1998.

Thanks to these diligent efforts, things were looking up for successful polio eradication in India. However, in August of 2002, polio cases in India tripled in the first half of the year compared with the same period one year earlier. Scientists estimate that this reappearance of the disease could set back the WHO's goal to 2005.

Of course, one must remember that the numbers are actually very small. A total of 480 new cases of polio were reported worldwide in 2001. More than half of these were in India. In 2002, India had 86 new cases between January and June of 2002. The Indian Health Department expected the numbers to increase in the second half of the year when polio normally increases due to the rainy season.

DID YOU KNOW THAT . . .

Dr. Matthias Gromeier at Duke University in North Carolina has created a genetically engineered poliovirus capable of destroying brain cells associated with a tumor known as malignant glioma. This tumor is the most common type of brain tumor in humans and is almost always fatal because it responds poorly to all types of therapy.

Dr. Gromeier inserted a piece of genetic material from a rhinovirus <RYE-no-virus> into a poliovirus. Rhinovirus is responsible for the common cold. Although the new, mixed polio/rhinovirus was unable to cause polio, it had a strong ability to attack and destroy the glioma cells in the brain. The tests were performed on mice and showed that only one treatment was needed to completely destroy any tumor cells.[13]

Polio has also made its reappearance in another area of the world. In October 2002, 27 children in the state of Kaduna, Nigeria, developed new cases of polio. Kaduna had not reported a single case of polio for the two previous years. In fact, the nation reported 113 new cases of the 720 reported worldwide by October. It is one of the countries worst hit by polio. The outbreak prompted a new vaccination drive in an effort to stop any further spread of the disease.

HOW WILL THE FUTURE OF POLIO CHANGE?

Now, the question is just how will this affect the future of the polio eradication project? Certainly, the increase in the number of new cases, small as it is, means that the eradication program is not moving along as fast as world health leaders and the WHO had hoped. Of course, a further improvement in the

---

13. Sliwa, Jim. "Genetically Engineered Poliovirus Fights Brain Tumors." *http://www.netbiosciencenews.com/NR/2001/June01/poliovirus061901.htm*

surveillance of the vaccination program will help to slow down and eventually stop the new cases from occurring.

Thanks to an amazing amount of cooperation between government officials, the World Health Organization, financial institutions, and the public itself, polio is close to global eradication. However, scientists have made several predictions concerning the future of this goal.

As already mentioned, Sabin's oral polio vaccine is made with attenuated virus. This means that the virus, although weakened, is still alive. This allows for the possibility of reversion back to the active or **virulent** <VEER-u-lent> form of the virus that can infect people. This reversion may come about through mutation (a spontaneous change in the virus' DNA) or by recombination with other forms of the virus that would provide the necessary genetic information to become active once again.

If this reversion occurs in a person who has been vaccinated, he or she may spread the virus through their feces and never know that they were passing it along. After all, they were vaccinated and developed antibodies, so they would not develop any symptoms. In such a case, they would be referred to as a *healthy carrier.*

WHERE DOES POLIO STILL EXIST?

Although there has been great success worldwide in eradicating polio, the virus is still quite active in India, Asia, sub-Saharan Africa, and several republics of the former Soviet Union (Figure 8.3). The reasons for this activity are due to poor sanitation and overcrowding. In addition, in many of these areas, children are not regularly vaccinated.

The increasing rate of international travel also contributes to the possible spread of polio. When a traveler visits one of these endemic areas (places where the disease normally exists), he or she may easily carry live virus back to the now "clean" Western world. This still poses a threat.

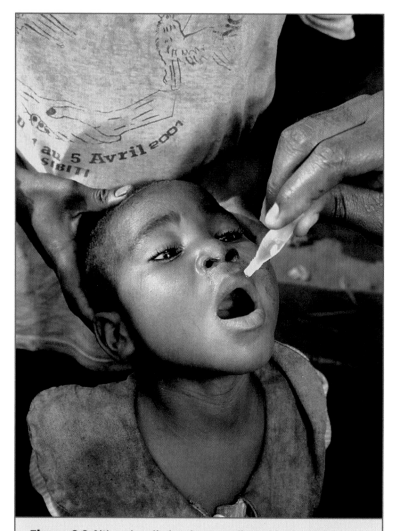

Figure 8.3 Although polio has been eradicated in the United States, it still exists in India, sub-Saharan Africa, and some areas of Eastern Europe. The World Health Organization and the Global Polio Eradication Initiative are attempting to fully eradicate polio from the earth by the year 2005. They plan to do this through a mass immunization program with the oral polio vaccine. The young African boy pictured here is receiving the oral polio vaccine, which has already dramatically decreased the number of polio cases in Africa.

WHEN WILL IT ALL END?

In order for polio to be considered totally eradicated from the face of the earth, the Global Polio Eradication Initiative has established specific requirements. The first step is containment of the virus, which has four parts: [14, 15]

1. National authorities in all countries survey laboratories to identify those with wild poliovirus infectious or potentially infectious materials and encourage destruction of all unneeded materials.

2. Laboratories retaining such materials institute enhanced biosafety level-2 procedures. This means that (A) laboratory personnel have specific training in handling pathogenic agents and are directed by competent scientists; (B) access to the laboratory is limited when work is being conducted; (C) extreme precautions are taken with contaminated sharp items; and (D) certain procedures in which infectious aerosols or splashes may be created are conducted in biological safety cabinets or other physical containment equipment.

3. National authorities develop a national inventory of all laboratories with wild poliovirus materials.

4. Member states begin planning for implementation of biosafety requirements for the post-eradication phase.

The second step is certification. This is the independent verification of wild poliovirus eradication. The WHO established a Global Certification Commission in 1995. This commission studies all aspects of the eradication program and determines

---

14. Global Polio Eradication Initiative
   www.polioeradication.org.

15. World Health Organization, Polio Eradication Information
   http://www.who.int/vaccines-polio/all/news/files/pdf/GlobalActionPlan_2nd.pdf

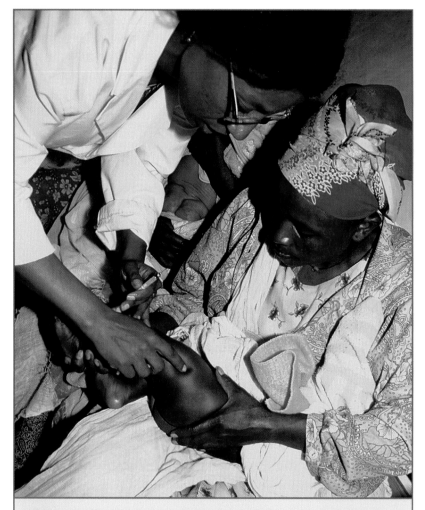

Figure 8.4 The Global Polio Eradication Initiative has established four steps towards the eradication of polio: immunization with the oral vaccine, booster vaccines to ensure continued immunity, "mop-up campaigns" to prevent transmission of the virus from those who already have it to those who may not have full immunity, and continued surveillance of areas where polio may still be present in some forms (for example, polioviruses in the water supply or non-symptomatic carriers). Since 50 percent of polio cases affect children under the age of three, it is especially important that this group receives immunizations, such as the young Ethiopian boy pictured above.

whether or not polio has, indeed, been eradicated from the earth. This will happen when three years have elapsed with zero new cases of wild poliovirus infection.

The third step is to establish a post-eradication immunization policy. This policy will be determined by the WHO member states. Information will include the amount of vaccine on hand throughout the world, production capacity, and potential costs of making more vaccine (Figure 8.4).

One last consideration relating to the future of polio is that of terrorism. In light of the many recent occurrences of terrorist acts throughout the world and the specific question of bioterrorism, many have asked whether or not polio might be one of the viruses that terrorist could use to threaten the earth.

Scientists agree that the largest viral threat is that of smallpox, a disease that has been eradicated from the earth thanks to an extensive vaccination program worldwide. They believe that polio, although a possible threat, is very low on the list of viruses to be concerned about.

Glossary

Acute—Having a rapid onset and following a short but severe course.

Antibody—A protein on the surface of B cells (one form of white blood cells) that is secreted into the blood or lymph in response to an antigenic stimulus, such as a bacterium, virus, parasite, or transplanted organ, and that neutralizes the antigen by binding specifically to it.

Anamnestic—A secondary response of the immune system, it occurs when the immune system recognizes an antigen to which it has already formed antibodies.

Antigen—A substance that, when introduced into the body, stimulates the production of an antibody. Antigens include toxins, bacteria, foreign blood cells, and the cells of transplanted organs.

Aseptic—Free of pathogenic microorganisms. Usually refers to the absence of bacteria as opposed to the absence of viruses.

Aseptic meningitis—Another name for nonparalytic polio.

Asymptomatic—Not showing any symptoms of a disease.

Attenuate—To weaken.

Biopsy—The removal and examination of a sample of tissue from a living body for diagnostic purposes.

Bioterrorism—The use of biological agents, such as pathogenic organisms or agricultural pests, for terrorist purposes.

Carrier—A person or an animal that shows no symptoms of a disease but harbors the infectious agent of that disease and is capable of transmitting it to others.

Disease—A pathological condition of a part, organ, or system of an organism resulting from various causes, such as infection, genetic defect, or environmental stress, and characterized by an identifiable group of signs or symptoms.

Epidemic—When a disease spreads rapidly and extensively by infection and affects many individuals in an area or a population at the same time.

Formaldehyde—A colorless compound used in embalming fluids and as a preservative and disinfectant.

Immobilization—To fix the position of a joint or limb, as with a splint or cast, so that it can no be moved.

Inflammation—A localized, protective reaction of tissue to irritation, injury, or infection. Characterized by pain, redness, swelling, and sometimes loss of function.

Influenza—An acute contagious viral infection characterized by inflammation of the respiratory tract and by fever, chills, muscular pain, and prostration.

Leukocyte—A type of white blood cell; part of the body's immune system.

Lymphocyte—Part of the immune system; one of the several types of white blood cells produced by humans which act to remove foreign organisms from the body; divided into B and T lymphocytes that are both essential to proper immune function.

Macrophage—One of the several types of white blood cells in humans; a large cell that seeks out and engulfs foreign particles and cells through phagocytosis; part of the human body's immune system.

Medulla oblongata—a portion of the brain stem; controls breathing and other vital functions, such as circulation of the blood.

Microbiology—The branch of biology that deals with microorganisms and their effects on other living organisms.

Microorganism—An organism of microscopic or submicroscopic size, especially a bacterium, virus or protozoan.

Mode of transmission—The mechanism by which a disease is passed from one person to another.

Neutrophil—Part of the body's immune system; a type of white blood cell that rids the body of foreign invaders through the process of phagocytosis.

Paralysis—Loss or impairment of the ability to move a body part, usually as a result of damage to its nerve supply.

Phagocytosis—The process by which a white blood cell engulfs and literally "eats" a foreign body.

Replicate—To reproduce or make an exact copy or copies.

Spasm—A sudden, involuntary contraction of a muscle or group of muscles.

Subunit vaccine—A type of vaccine created by isolating specific antigens or parts of antigens of the foreign substance and introducing these into the body to form anibodies.

Symptom—A sign or an indication of disorder or disease, especially when experienced by an individual as a change from normal function, sensation, or appearance.

Syndrome—A group of symptoms that collectively indicate or characterize a disease, psychological disorder, or other abnormal condition.

Tetanus—A type of bacterial disease that causes muscle spasms and paralysis.

Toxoid—A substance that has been treated to destroy its toxic properties but retains the capacity to stimulate production of antitoxins, used in immunization.

Virulent—Capable of causing disease by breaking down protective mechanisms of the host.

Bibliography

Associated Press. "Setback in the War on Polio." *Newsday* (August 13, 2002): A16.

Cooke, Robert. "A Virus Made from Scratch." *Newsday* (July 12, 2002): A8, A49.

Halstead, Lauro. *Managing Post-Polio Syndrome: A Guide to Living Well With Post-Polio Syndrome*. Arlington, Va.: ABI Professional Publishers, 1998.

Paul, John. *A History of Poliomyelitis*. New Haven, Conn.: Yale University Press, 1971.

Sass, Edmund. *Polio's Legacy: An Oral History*. Lanham, Md.: University of America Press, 1996.

Alan Alda Biography
http://www.geocities.com/Athens/oracle/2515/xkane.html

Albert Sabin Biography
http://www.us-israel.org/jsource/biography/Sabin.html

Eckard Wimmer
http://www.rfsuny.org/research_spotlight/wimmer.htm

Emperor Claudius Biography, Ancient/Classical History at *about.com*
http://ancienthistory.about.com

Epidemiology of Polio
http://cumicro2.cpmc.columbia.edu/PICO/Chapters/Epidemiology.html

Edward Jenner Biography
http://www.sc.edu/library/spcoll/nathist/jenner1.html

Famous People With Polio
http://www.geocities.com/HotSprings/4760/pprg_famous.html

FDR's Disability
http://www.hmcnet.harvard.edu/pmr/fdr.html

Fear of Polio in the 1950s
http://www.inform.umd.edu/HONR/HONR269J/.WWW/projects/sokol.html

History of FDR's Polio
http://www.feri.org/archives/polio/default.cfm

How a Virus Works (boxed feature)
http://www.howstuffworks.com/virus-human.htm

How to Make a Vaccine
http://www.pbs.org/wgbh/nova/bioterror/vaccines.html

Jonas Salk Information
http://www.achievement.org/autodoc/page/sal0bio-1

Jonas Salk Biography at *Top-Biography.com*
http://www.top-biography.com/9027-Jonas%20Salk/life.htm

Polio History
http://medicine.wustl.edu/~virology/lio.htm

Polio in Afghanistan
http://www.afghan-web.com/articles/poliomy.html

Poliomyelitis and the New Polio Vaccine
http://hscconcord.tamu.edu/medmicro_pages/polio.htm

Polio Timeline
http://www.cloudnet.com/~edrbsass/poliotimeline.htm

Post-Polio Research Group
http://www.geocities.com/HotSprings/4760/pprg_faq.html

Post-Polio Syndrome History
http://www.ott.zynet.co.uk/polio/lincolnshire/library/halstead/sciampps.html

Quote from Presidential Medal of Freedom Ceremony
http://www.reagan.utexas.edu/resource/speeches/1986/51286b.htm

Sabin Vaccine Information
http://www.cincypost.com/living/sabin070899.html

Sister Kenny Quote
http://www.ott.zynet.co.uk/polio/lincolnshire/library/drhenry/srkenny.html

Statistics of Vaccine Trials
http://www.pbs.org/wgbh/aso/databank/entries/dm52sa.html

Transmission of Polio
http://www.brown.edu/Courses/Bio_160/Projects1999/polio/polweb.html

The University of Leicester, Department of Microbiology and Immunology
http://www-micro.msb.le.ac.uk

Wilma Rudolph Biography
http://www.lkwdpl.org/wihohio/rudo-wil.htm

Further Reading

Bredeson, Carmen. *Jonas Salk: Discoverer of the Polio Vaccine.* Hillside, N.J.: Enslow Press, 1993.

Burge, Michael, and Don Nardo. *Vaccines: Preventing Disease.* San Diego, Cal.: Lucent Books, 1992.

Cowie, Peter. *Coppola.* New York: Scribner, 1990.

Dolan, Edward. *Jenner and the Miracle of Vaccine.* New York: Dodd, Mead, 1960.

Farrow, Mia. *What Falls Away: A Memoir.* New York: Nan A. Tavese, 1997.

Gould, Jean. *A Good Fight: The Story of F.D.R.'s Conquest of Polio.* New York: Dodd, Mead, 1960.

Kenny, Elizabeth. *And They Shall Walk: The Life Story of Sister Elizabeth Kenny.* New York: Dodd, 1943.

Marx, Joseph. *Keep Trying: A Practical Book for the Handicapped.* New York: Hagan and Rowe, 1974.

McDonough, Jimmy. *Shakey: Neil Young's Biography.* New York: Villard Books, 2002.

Rains, A.J. Harding. *Edward Jenner and Vaccination.* London: Priory Press, 1974.

Rosenberg, Nancy and Louis Cooper. *Vaccines and Viruses.* New York: Grosset and Dunlap, 1971.

Seavey, Nina G., Jane Smith, and Paul Wagner. *A Paralyzing Fear: The Triumph Over Polio in America.* New York: TV Books, 1998.

Strait, Raymond. *Alan Alda: A Biography.* New York: St. Martin's Press, 1983.

Tomlinson, Michael. *Jonas Salk.* Vero Beach, Fla.: Rourke Publications, 1993.

Weaver, Lydia. *Close to Home: A Story of the Polio Epidemic.* New York: Viking Press, 1993.

Websites

Centers for Disease Control and Prevention
http://www.cdc.gov

Development of Polio Vaccines
http://www.accessexcellence.org/AE/AEC/CC/polio.html

Information on Albert Sabin
http://www.cincinnatichildrens.org/Research/About/History/sabin.htm

Information on Jonas Salk
http://www.achievement.org/autodoc/page/sal0bio-1

Polio Eradication
http://www.polioeradication.org/

Polio Experience Network
http://www.polionet.org/

Post-Polio Syndrome Central
http://www.skally.net/ppsc/

World Health Organization
http://www.who.int

Index

Picture Credits

About the Author

Dr. Alan Hecht is a practicing chiropractor in New York. He is also an adjunct associate professor at Farmingdale State University, Nassau Community College, and at the C.W. Post campus of Long Island University. He teaches courses in medical microbiology, anatomy and physiology, comparative anatomy, embryology, and general biology.

In addition, Dr. Hecht is a full-time high school teacher at Lawrence Woodmere Academy in Woodmere, N.Y., where he teaches anatomy, genetics, psychology, and chemistry.

About the Editor

The late **I. Edward Alcamo** was a Distinguished Teaching Professor of Microbiology at the State University of New York at Farmingdale. Alcamo studied biology at Iona College in New York and earned his M.S. and Ph.D. degrees in microbiology at St. John's University, also in New York. He taught at Farmingdale for over 30 years. In 2000, Alcamo won the Carski Award for Distinguished Teaching in Microbiology, the highest honor for microbiology teachers in the United States. He was a member of the American Society for Microbiology, the National Association of Biology Teachers, and the American Medical Writers Association. Alcamo authored numerous books on the subjects of microbiology, AIDS, and DNA technology as well as the award-winning textbook *Fundamentals of Microbiology*, now in its sixth edition.